GENESIS
AND THE
DECAY OF THE NATIONS

BY
KEN HAM

CREATION SCIENCE FOUNDATION LTD.
BRISBANE, AUSTRALIA

MASTER BOOKS PUBLISHERS
EL CAJON, CALIFORNIA

1991

D0089242

GENESIS AND THE DECAY OF THE NATIONS

Copyright ©1991 Ken Ham

Published by

CREATION SCIENCE FOUNDATION LTD.
P.O. BOX 302
SUNNYBANK, QLD, 4109, AUSTRALIA
(07) 273 7650

MASTER BOOKS PUBLISHERS
P.O. BOX 1606
EL CAJON, CALIFORNIA 92022
(619) 448-1121

Library of Congress Catalog Card Number 91-72185
ISBN 0-932766-23-4

Copy Editing: Barbara Hight
Cover Artwork: Marvin Ross
Illustrations: Steve Cardno
Art Direction: Ron Hight

Printed in the United States of America

Dedication

The Lord has entrusted five beautiful children to my wife, Mally, and me. It is our prayer that Nathan, Renee, Danielle, Jeremy, and Kristel will grow in the Lord daily, as we endeavor to build their lives on the correct foundation.

"Lo, children are an heritage of the Lord" (Psalm 127:3). As parents, we need to be diligent in carrying out the enormous responsibility given to us by the Lord to train for Him the precious lives he has put into our care.

This book is dedicated to our five children, whose individual personalities are a continual reminder of how hard we must work in our own family to build the correct foundation. We pray that this book will not only encourage other parents to build their family on the foundation of God's Word, but will also help them recognize the foundational nature of the battles occurring around the world by those bent on destroying family and nation.

Acknowledgments

From my perspective, one sad aspect of writing a book is that the words do not have my Australian accent! Nonetheless, the way I write is basically the way I speak. Thus, anything I write has a conversational style. Even so, it has taken many hours of editing by a number of special people to make this book what it is.

I would like to thank Dr. Henry Morris (president of the Institute for Creation Research), Julie Hayes, from Texas (long-time supporter of the creation ministry), Dr. Carl Wieland (managing director of the Creation Science Foundation in Australia), and Joy Rizor (my secretary and "Back to Genesis" seminar organizer at ICR — and adopted as Aunty Joy by our five children) for the editorial skills they applied to this work.

Sincere appreciation is also expressed to Sonia Swanson (a secretary with the Creation Science Foundation Ltd.) for the many times she typed the manuscript.

I consider it a great honor that the president and founder of ICR, Dr. Henry Morris, a man with a real talent for writing and the author of most of the classic works that have been published on the creation/evolution issue, has written the foreword for this book. Dr. Morris is not only a friend (and my boss), but is the one whom the Lord used through his research and writing to bring me into full-time work in the creation ministry in Australia, and now in the USA.

ICR's artist, Marvin Ross, designed and painted the cover of my first book, *The Lie: Evolution*. This had such an impact that I asked him to produce the cover for this book.

The illustrations through the book were drawn by the CSF artist in Australia, Steve Cardno. Steve's cartoon style has contributed greatly to the success of the many illustrated talks I give at our seminars.

My close friend at ICR, Mr. Don Rohrer (ICR's business manager), has used his invaluable talents and experience to oversee the production and printing of this book.

Foreword

The book of Genesis is the foundation book of the Bible and, therefore, of all Christian faith and life. The founding fathers of our nation understood this, and recognized the God of Creation as the author of all true liberty and righteousness in human affairs.

But our nation has been moved off its foundation as a direct result of pervasive evolutionary teaching, and is in real danger of moral and spiritual disintegration. Our government, our schools — even our churches — urgently need to be called back to the Bible, and this means back to Genesis, first of all. Most of the other nations of the world, including Ken Ham's native Australia, have drifted even farther away from the wise and loving Creator/Redeemer who "determined the times before appointed, and the bounds of their habitation" (Acts 17:26).

It was barely four years ago that the Lord led Ken Ham from Australia to America, but in that short time he has brought his "Back to Genesis" messages to many, many thousands in all parts of the country. After Australia's Creation Science Foundation was started there, in his own living room, he led in the establishment of a remarkably successful creation ministry in that great continent "down under." But then, realizing the key role of the United States in the world's economy, including especially the global witness of its Bible-believing churches and missions, he became convinced the Lord would have him move here, believing that his message would have even greater worldwide impact if it were centered here.

That God was, indeed, really leading him in this move has been abundantly confirmed. He joined our ICR staff in December 1986, and soon began to organize our "Back to Genesis" seminars. These have now reached many thousands in each of many key cities, and are contributing greatly to the modern revival of creationism in churches and schools all across America.

One of his most effective lectures in these seminars has been an impassioned message entitled "Genesis and the Decay of the Nations." This book is an adaptation and enlargement of that message. Combining Bible principles and scientific truth in his own inimitable, down-to-earth style, the book manifests the same deep concern and sincere spiritual dedication that characterize his spoken messages.

Ken Ham is uncompromising in biblical integrity. He has a quick mind, keen sense of humor, genuine love of family, and unsurpassed zeal in the ministry.

I trust this book, calling our nation and other nations back to their true foundations in the creative purpose of God, will reach many hearts and change many lives.

Henry M. Morris
Institute for Creation Research

Contents

Chapter One — Did God Really Say That?
Doubt — that insidious and insinuating thing that can ultimately lead to unbelief. Doubt concerning the book of Genesis has caused many Christians to eventually distrust much of the rest of the Bible.

Chapter Two — The Genesis Foundation
This chapter basically summarizes the material in the book *The Lie: Evolution*. All major biblical doctrines, directly or indirectly, have their foundation in the book of Genesis. To understand Christianity fully, one has to believe and understand the book of Genesis.

Chapter Three — From Darkness to Light
Opinion-oriented philosophy pervades our church today. People's opinions basically determine "truth." We need a reformation in the church as in the days of Martin Luther. We must return to the proper foundation of our faith — the infallible, inerrant Word of God.

Chapter Four — The Compromise Road
Theistic evolution, "gap theory," and other compromise positions have resulted from the attempts of Christians to reinterpret the Bible on the basis of the fallible theories of scientists. These compromise positions ultimately lead to destruction.

Chapter Five — Christianity is Unique

One cannot use science to PROVE the Bible is true. It does require faith to accept God's Word, but it is not blind faith. There is plenty of evidence to substantiate this faith. The evidence for the global flood of Noah's day, the evidence for creation, the explanation of the races — the evidence overwhelmingly fits with what the Bible states. Christianity is not a blind faith. The evidence is real and convincing, at least to a person who does not willfully resist it.

Chapter Six — The Path to Destruction

The bloodbath of the French Revolution resulted because a foundation consistent with humanist reasoning had been laid down in society. About the same time, the nation of England saw Christian revival, because a different foundation had been built. Something akin to the French Revolution is occurring today in nations around the world, because the foundation of Christianity is being eroded.

Chapter Seven — Foundation for Family and Nation

Satan used the same method of creating doubt in Eve's mind as he did to create doubt about the book of Genesis. This doubt ultimately led to unbelief, and thus the destruction of the foundation of God's Word. The barrier against humanism was being destroyed.

Chapter Eight — The Erosion of Genesis

The subtle undermining of Genesis was continued in earnest by James Hutton and Charles Lyell. Because of their work, the concept of "uniformitarianism" was popularized. They helped create an environment that paved the way for the acceptance of Charles Darwin's ideas.

Chapter Nine — The Pyramid Effect

Christian leaders, including many theologians, began to compromise between evolutionary ideas and the Bible. These leaders then taught their students, who eventually taught their own congregations, to compromise Genesis with evolution. Eventually, most of the church rejected a literal Genesis.

Chapter Ten — The Generation Gap

Scientists are now recognizing that they have no mechanism to explain how evolution works. What they say is something like, "We know evolution occurs, we just don't know how it occurs!" They need an outside intelligence to explain life, but they won't entertain belief in the God of the Bible. However, they are allowing "New Age" mysticism as a substitute for God.

Chapter Eleven — Restoration, Reconstruction and Revival

The church needs revival. Reconstruction of the Christian framework can happen only if the foundation for this framework is restored in society. Because of the compromise in the church, this restoration needs to start with God's people. Revival must begin in the church. The church needs to get back to Genesis.

Introduction

The first major book I wrote, *The Lie: Evolution*, was written while I was living in Australia, and was published by Master Books in California, USA. *Genesis and the Decay of the Nations* is really a sequel to *The Lie*.

In my book *The Lie*, I show how important it is for Christians to accept a literal Genesis. Sadly, many Christians have been led to believe that it doesn't matter whether one takes the Genesis account literally or not. Also, probably the majority of those attending church think that it is permissible to accept evolution as the way God created, or accept the basic evolutionary time-scale of billions of years. In *The Lie*, I pointed out how foundational Genesis was to the rest of the Bible, and thus to all doctrine. I also insisted that if one accepts the basic evolutionary tenets of death for millions of years before man, then the foundation of the message of the cross has been destroyed. I challenged Christians to get back to an unyielding and steadfast acceptance of the Genesis account, and reject any compromise with the evolutionary theories proposed by man.

In this new book, *Genesis and the Decay of the Nations*, I explain what happened historically to cause people to begin to doubt the book of Genesis. The onset of this doubt was the result of the idea that the geologic record, containing numerous layers of rock with billions of fossils, was not formed from catastrophism associated with the flood of Noah's day, but was the result of millions of years of slow processes.

Thus, people began to reject the idea of a global flood, and thousands of years for the earth's time-scale. This doubt paved the way for Darwin to popularize evolutionary concepts that led many Christians to totally reject a literal Genesis. As a result of this rejection, the foundations of the Christian faith began to crumble. As the foundation crumbled, so did the structure (Christianity) that was built on this foundation. Consequently the Christian fabric of society and the Christian family structure began to collapse.

Today, most Christian colleges and seminaries reject taking what Genesis says in a straightforward manner. Most refuse to accept that God created everything in six literal days, that the flood of Noah was global, that physical death and bloodshed came only after Adam sinned, and that the world is only thousands of years old.

When one looks at families and schools today, it is easy to see that those that began with a Christian structure, but rejected the foundation of Genesis, have now by-and-large disintegrated to a "Christianized secular," or downright pagan, structure. The popularization of Darwinian evolution is one of the strongest forces today that is destroying families and nations.

Many, particularly the leading theologians, mock those who even suggest that the universe is not billions of years old, but perhaps only thousands. However, the reason it sounds so radical to believe in a young age for the earth and universe is not because the geological and cultural history of this planet cannot be explained within a framework of only thousands of years, but because the education system and media have successfully indoctrinated the population to believe in terms of millions, or billions, of years. To believe otherwise is considered on a par with believing in a flat earth!

This book explains how the undermining of the book of Genesis began in our modern society, and facilitates the subsequent destruction of family and nation. Understanding the creation/evolution issue is paramount to understanding where the real battle is in our society.

Many are calling for revival in our nations, but revival can occur only if the foundation on which to build it is secure. We need to restore the foundation of creation in family and nation, so the Christian structure can withstand the forces of evil.

Chapter **1** # Did God Really Say That?

I had been invited to present the case for creation to the science classes at a major public high school. The audience of teachers and students was mostly non-Christian. I spoke for fifty minutes, dealing with the limitations of science, and the evidence which supported a belief in creation and a worldwide flood. Some of the students then asked if I were really talking about the Bible. These questions, of course, gave me a wonderful opportunity to discuss spiritual things, because I had shown that evolution is a belief, and that there is overwhelming evidence for a creator; the groundwork had now been laid to give me some credibility.

One of the questions which always seems to come up was asked by a teacher: "Why can't a person believe in both evolution and the Genesis account of origins?" I explained that to do so would be inconsistent, because the Bible teaches that death came into the world only after Adam sinned. Evolutionists, on the other hand, claim that death and bloodshed existed on the earth for millions of years before the appearance of man. (These ideas are discussed in more detail in **Chapter 2**.)

I was then asked why I felt this topic was so important. I replied that what we believe about where we came from affects our entire world view. For exam-

1

ple, if there is no God, and all life has evolved by chance random processes, then there is no one to whom we are accountable. On the other hand, if there **is** a God, then we are accountable to Him because He created us. I also stated that Christians must defend the book of Genesis, since all biblical doctrines are, in one way or another, founded in this first book of the Bible — the book of beginnings. Its historicity is vital to the foundation and structure of Christianity. (This point is discussed in detail in my book *The Lie: Evolution*, and summarized in Chapter 2 of this book.)

The same teacher then very thoughtfully asked, "Why is it, then, that the church does not defend Genesis? Why do so many leaders in the Christian world believe in evolution? If the creation versus evolution topic is so important, why don't we see the church making an issue of it in society? Why does the church have doubts about a literal Genesis?" Good questions!

It is true that many people in the Christian world today have doubts about the book of Genesis. Often these doubts lead to full-blown disbelief in the truths of this fundamental portion of Scripture. In II Corinthians 11:3, Paul sounds a warning which I believe directly relates to this matter: "But I fear, lest by any means, as the serpent beguiled Eve through his subtilty, so your minds should be corrupted from the simplicity that is in Christ." His point is that Satan will use the same method today that he did with Eve, to bring us to a point of unbelief. This method,

2

used throughout the ages, is at once both subtle and extremely effective. It is a psychological approach which can cause Christians to exchange their long-cherished beliefs for "new" and unscriptural ideas. It is a very simple method which is being used daily on Christians. What is this ingenious method? **Creating doubt!**

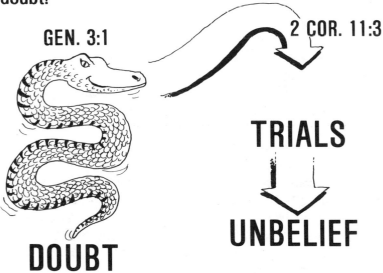

GEN. 3:1

2 COR. 11:3

TRIALS

UNBELIEF

DOUBT

Doubt can lead to unbelief. It is an insidious and insinuating thing. For instance, when tragedies come into our lives, it is easy for us to succumb to doubt concerning God's Word and what it says about His care for us. This doubt often leads to outright unbelief — a total rejection of God. This is the sort of thing Paul is warning us about. Satan tries to create doubt, knowing that, ultimately, doubt will lead to unbelief. The way he accomplished this with Eve was by making her consider the question,

"Did God really say that?" Once Eve began to doubt, she next questioned God's directive not to eat the fruit of the tree of the knowledge of good and evil. She and Adam then chose not to believe God's warning. Doubt had led directly to disbelief, and disbelief had led directly to disobedience.

Actually, Satan misquoted what God had said. He tricked Eve with a half-truth. It is so easy to twist someone's words and undermine their integrity. I have seen this happen in churches. A pastor who is a good Bible teacher and a devout Christian with a fruitful ministry can be systematically destroyed by certain people in the congregation who begin to introduce doubts about what he is preaching, or about his motives. Others then become convinced that he is really preaching at them personally, or that there are hidden meanings in his sermons. Before long, enough doubt has been created that many no longer support him, and he is forced either to move or quit the ministry entirely — all because of doubt: subtle and destructive doubt.

Sadly, many churchgoers and Christian leaders no longer believe in either the literal truth or the importance of Genesis (particularly Chapters 1-11). In fact, Scriptural unbelief is rampant in our churches. Many no longer even believe in the miracles such as the Parting of the Red Sea, the Virgin Birth, and the Resurrection. What has caused such unbelief — such a departure from the teachings of men like John Wesley, and the reformers, Martin Luther, or Calvin?

4

I recall an incident that occured when I was speaking to a group of pastors on "The Relevance of Creation." One young and obviously very bright and committed pastor took exception to what I had said. As I talked with him, I discovered that, although he really did believe the basic doctrines of Christianity, he did not feel that the book of Genesis was any more than simply a picture for the Hebrews, containing some truth about Creation. So I asked him how we know that we are sinners. He said it was obvious to him by just looking at himself. I told him that his perception might be wrong, so how did he ultimately know? He could not answer. I told him I know because Romans 5:12-14 tells me I have inherited the sin nature of Adam. I explained that, because of the literal event of the eating of the forbidden fruit, and the consequent entrance of sin, we are therefore all sinners, as the Apostle Paul so eloquently explains in Romans, Chapter 5.

He realized that all doctrine originated in Genesis, but he did not think that it was necessary to accept the book as literal and historical. He tried to explain that we somehow must ascertain the meaning of Genesis. I then asked him to tell me just what it did mean. He admitted he wasn't sure. He knew he believed that Jesus died on a cross and rose from the dead, because the Bible said so. He knew that Genesis said God took dust and made a man, but he did not know what this meant, because it was teaching some truth for the Hebrews! His confusion was very obvious.

Finally, we turned the conversation to something more specific. He told me that many of the children in his church had questions about Creation, Genesis, and evolution. I asked him how he had explained fossils, for instance — where they came from, and how they fit into history. He did not know what to do with them. He said one would have to look at the fossils to determine what might have happened.

I explained that in Genesis, God has revealed to us that the ancient world was inundated by a global flood. We are told that death came only after Adam sinned (Romans 5:12). I reasoned that if these things were true, they would have great ramifications in our understanding of geology, and specifically in such things as fossil formation. For example, layers of rock containing animal fossils (preserved

6

remains of animals) could not have been formed before the first man sinned (which brought death), and must thus be explained by processes which occurred **after** Adam's rebellion, such as Noah's Flood. Thus, he could have given the children in his church a logical answer, supported by evidence, to help them understand that the Bible (God's Word) is the basis of all true science. Although the young pastor had no answer for them, the children's evolutionist teachers certainly would — an answer which would surely create doubt, and ultimately unbelief, in the truths of Genesis.

I further asked this young man to tell me who had taught him to doubt Genesis. "My seminary professors," he replied. Here was a confused young pastor, producing confusion in the minds of the people in his congregation because of his own great doubts about the book of Genesis. I told him that I could almost guarantee that many in his church (particularly among the children) who were being taught by him would doubt, not just Genesis, but gradually the rest of Scripture, and would, ultimately, disbelieve totally.

Sadly, most teachers in seminaries and Bible colleges have succumbed to Satan's subtle ploy concerning Genesis — **did God really say that?** Did God really say six days for Creation? Did God really mean Adam was the first man? Did God really mean a global flood? Did God really mean there was a tree of the knowledge of good and evil?

As I continued to talk with this pastor, something else became evident. He kept repeating that Genesis was written for the Hebrews and, thus, was not relevant for us today. But Genesis is a part of the Bible, and the Bible tells us over 3,000 times that all of Scripture is the Word of God. As Paul told the Thessalonians, it is the Word of God, **not** of men (I Thessalonians 2:13): "... when ye received the Word of God which ye heard of us, ye received it not as the word of men, but as it is in truth, the Word of God. ..." The Bible teaches that **all** Scripture (II Timothy 3:16) is inspired and will stand forever. God moved men by His Spirit to write **His words.** If it is not the Word of God, then we can never be sure what truth is. God communicates to us through His written Word. It seems that many, like the pastor above, have succumbed to another doubt from Satan: Is the Bible really God's Word? Does God really mean what He says?

A young woman called Pat, and her family, are sad examples of how doubt can destroy lives. She and her husband were educated in church schools, and brought up in the church. As adults, they no longer attended church, and argued vehemently against the Bible and Christianity. I was introduced to them at a meeting in a private home to which they had been specially invited. They came out of curiosity to hear someone speak about Creation, and they listened intently. At the end of the meeting, they brought up their favorite topic: the so-called "mistakes" in the Bible.

8

According to them, the Bible was full of errors from beginning to end. I tried my best to answer carefully each supposed "mistake," pointing out how they had either misread, taken out of context, or just plain misunderstood the various statements. After a considerable time, Pat stopped and said, "There is one event that occurred in my life that stands out more than any other." She explained that when she was in the ninth grade, Father Brown had told her class that there was a mistake in the Bible right from the beginning. He explained that in the first chapter of Genesis it says that God created man on the sixth day, but in the account of Creation in the second chapter of Genesis it says that He created man on the third day. Pat had not trusted the Bible since then. I asked her to show me in the Bible where this mistake occurred. She answered, "Oh, I don't know. I just took Father Brown's word for it." I showed her from the Bible that this supposed mistake did **not** exist. "And that means," I told her, "that Father Brown was wrong!" However, the damage had been done; doubt in regard to this first book of the Bible had led, ultimately, to unbelief.

Pat suffered from a problem which many have today — she had accepted what someone said about the Bible without searching the Scriptures herself to see if these things were so. When one studies the Bible diligently, it becomes increasingly evident that Genesis is foundational to the remainder of the Word of God.

2 The Genesis Foundation

Chapter

Even though you may already be familiar with the material in *The Lie: Evolution*, the information in this chapter will be a good review for you. We do need to be reminded of Scriptural truths. As Peter said, "... I will not be negligent to put you always in remembrance of these things, though ye know them, ..." (II Peter 1:12).

Genesis is one of the most disbelieved and attacked books of the Bible in both Christian and non-Christian circles. Yet, Genesis is the most quoted book in the Bible. Consider John 5:45-47, where Jesus Christ says, "Do not think that I will accuse you to the Father: there is one that accuseth you, even Moses in whom ye trust. For had ye believed Moses, ye would have believed Me: for he wrote of Me. But if ye believe not his writings, how shall ye believe My words?" In Luke 16:31, Jesus quoted Abraham as saying, "If they hear not Moses and the prophets, neither will they be persuaded, though one rose from the dead." In Luke 24:27 we read, "And beginning at Moses and all the prophets, He (Jesus) expounded unto them in all the Scriptures the things concerning Himself." At the end of Acts we read where Paul preached about Jesus Christ from Moses and the prophets.

Why is it then that one book of the writings of Moses — Genesis — is the most quoted and the most attacked?

Consider the foundation of a structure such as a house. If the foundation is destroyed, then the structure will no longer stand. The psalmist asks, "If the foundations be destroyed, what can the righteous do?" (Psalm 11:3). Now, think about our nation. From a Christian perspective, the moral fabric (Christian structure) is collapsing. The family unit is also collapsing. The two are very much interrelated, because the family is the backbone of the nation. The structures are collapsing simply because the foundations are being eroded. Let's study these foundations and see just what is happening.

Many church-going people appear to be ignorant of the fact that all Christian doctrine is founded in the book of Genesis. Virtually every (some would say every) single doctrine of theology, directly or indirectly, has its foundation in the first book of the Bible.

The meaning of anything is related to its origin. The meaning of marriage, for instance, is based in the book of Genesis, the book which gives us the first historical account of marriage. This is also true of death, sin, the seven-day week, why we wear clothes, and why Jesus died on a cross — all doctrine ultimately has its foundation in the book of Genesis, some more directly than others. Even the relationship between Christ and His Church is related

12

to Adam and Eve by Paul, as he wrote in Ephesians 5:31-32.

Logically then, the Christian framework (like its doctrine) can stand only when the foundation exists. But if the foundation is removed, then the entire Christian structure will ultimately collapse.

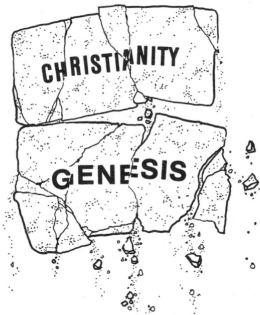

Christian parents want the Christian structure to be built into the next generation — their children. However, if they attempt to build this framework without the proper foundation, it will not easily stand. There are whole generations of Christian families in which the children are rebelling against Christianity, and in which the structure is collapsing.

13

Although a house cannot be built from the roof down, many Christians attempt to build a Biblical structure in the next generation in this way, instead of from the foundation up. Sadly, children from these homes often attend public schools where they are taught that evolution is the foundation, as opposed to the Genesis Creation foundation. And many of these children ultimately totally reject Christianity, so the structure collapses. Many parents have noticed that the decline in their children's interest in Christianity has gone hand-in-hand with the increased teaching of evolution in public schools and colleges. So what is the bottom-line issue when it comes to these two different foundations of creation and evolution?

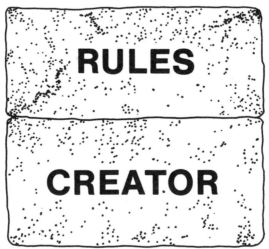

1. **Creation.** The fact that there is a Creator means that He owns everything, including each person. He has total claim on our lives and has a right to set the rules. He can tell us what is right and wrong,

because He is the Creator, the absolute authority. We can know what is good and bad, because there is one who is good and who can therefore define right and wrong. All humans need to submit themselves totally to the one who owns them. Nothing in life is merely a matter of human opinion.

2. Evolution. In most instances, through the media and public education systems, this theory is taught to explain the origin of life. It is an anti-God religion which claims that humans are products of properties inherent in matter, and chance random processes over millions of years. It would logically follow that there is no absolute authority — no one owns you if you have simply evolved. People can then write their own rules, and have their own opinions about everything. There is no absolute authority who has a right to impose rules on anyone. Therefore, the more people believe that there is no God who owns them, the more each one will apply this in his own thinking, like the Israelites described in the book of Judges. There we are told that when they had no king to tell them what to do, "every man did that which was right in his own eyes." (Judges 21:25) As people abandon the Genesis foundation, they also abandon Christian doctrine.

Let us look in detail at three specific doctrines which originated in Genesis.

1. Marriage. In Matthew 19, we read that Jesus was asked about divorce. He answered the question

15

in verses 4 and 5, "Have ye not read, that He which made them at the beginning made them male and female, and said, For this cause shall a man leave father and mother, and shall cleave to his wife: and they twain shall be one flesh?" Jesus quoted from Genesis to give the foundation (and thus the reason) for marriage. Starting with the origin of marriage in Genesis, we learn a number of aspects concerning this doctrine:

a. **The Spiritual Meaning of the Marriage Tie.** God took dust and made man. He took part of the man's side and made woman. A husband and wife are **one** in marriage because man and woman were one flesh historically. If it weren't so historically, then the spiritual meaning of oneness is invalid. A man and a woman are to cleave unto each other as if they had no parents, just like Adam and Eve, who had no parents.

b. **The Origin of the Family Unit.** The family is founded upon a male and a female — one man for one woman for life. Why must marriage be between a male and a female, and not between two males or two females? Because God made man and woman and thus He set the standard. God instituted marriage, and gave the man and woman their separate roles. God made Adam and Eve — not two men or two women — as the basis for the first family in history. This is why Paul teaches that homosexuality is a perverse, anti-God practice; it destroys the family (Romans 1:26-27).

16

c. The Importance of Marriage. One of the primary concerns of marriage is found in Malachi 2:15. In the context of this passage, we understand that the Israelites had taken pagan wives, and brought idols into their homes. They were destroying the meaning of the family unit as God had ordained it. Through the prophet, God asked them why He originally made the two to become one (a reference to the creation of man and woman recorded in Genesis). He then answered that the reason was because He sought Godly offspring from their union. These Godly offspring were meant to influence the world for Jesus Christ, and produce similar offspring themselves. This should be the case generation after generation.

d. Roles. Concerning the roles of mother and father, it must be understood that God sets the rules because He is the Creator. He made marriage. Many husbands and wives follow their own ideas, rather than obeying the rules God has given for their roles in marriage. But for marriage to work, both the husband and the wife must be prepared to accept the roles ordained by God.

(1) Woman's Role. The Bible explicitly states that Adam was created first. Furthermore, Eve was deceived; therefore, a woman is to be in submission to her husband. Many women do not want to be in submission to their husbands. However, it is not a matter of one's opinion, but rather of obeying the rules God has given for marriage. In order for the children in the family to observe the example of the correct roles as a pattern for their own adult lives, their parents must obey the Bible. Unfortunately, some wives think that "submission" implies that a man is superior to a woman, but the Bible teaches that men and women are equal in God's sight. It is not a matter of equality, then, but of roles.

(2) Man's Role. The husband is told to love his wife as Christ loved the Church and gave Himself for it (Ephesians 5:25). Husbands must exhibit this type of love to their wives so their children can see it. There is another very special role for the husband and father; one which is not being obeyed in most Christian homes today. In Isaiah 38:19 we read that "the father to the children shall make known thy truth." Ephesians 6:4 states, "Fathers, bring your children up in the nurture and admonition of the Lord." It is obvious from many passages in both the Old and New Testaments that the father is to be the spiritual head of the house, instructing his children, and acting as a priest to his wife and family.

2. Clothing. Why do people wear clothes? If it is only because of fashion, convenience, or comfort related to the outside temperature, then the standards are whatever anyone makes them. In other words, if this issue is based merely on human opinion, then no one should be forced to wear clothes. However, the ultimate reason we wear clothes is because God gave them to us.

The origin of clothing is found in the book of Genesis. Because of Adam's action in eating the forbidden fruit, sin entered the world. Sin distorts everything, including nakedness. As a result of sin, God

19

gave Adam and Eve coats of animals' skins (Genesis 3:21) as the first blood sacrifice — a covering for their sin, and a picture of what was to come in the sacrificial death of the Lord Jesus Christ.

If God provided clothes because of sin, then it follows that there must be standards for clothing. In the New Testament this is made clear. We are told that if a man lusts after a woman in his heart, he commits adultery (Matthew 5:28). The reason men are singled out is because they respond sexually very easily to the sight of a woman's body. That is the way men were made. However, because of sin, this created feature has been distorted, and men now have the problem of lust. Even Job recognized this, for in Job 31:1, he says he made a covenant with his eyes so he would not think lustfully upon a maiden.

3. **The Gospel.** The foundation of the Gospel message is also in the book of Genesis. The Bible clearly teaches that death came into the world after Adam sinned (Romans 5:12-14), and not millions of years before man supposedly evolved. God then provided a means for man's deliverance because of sin. When man (in Adam) rebelled against God (the entrance of sin), he died immediately, in a spiritual sense. He was cut off from God, and would have remained so for eternity. But God provided a means by which man could be reconciled to Him.

In Hebrews 9:22 we read that "without shedding of blood there is no remission of sin." God introduced

20

death and bloodshed so that man could eventually be redeemed. (He necessarily killed at least one animal in the Garden of Eden in order to provide Adam and Eve with their coats of skin.) Death and bloodshed did not exist before Adam fell. In fact, if they had, the message of redemption would be nonsense. God, in love, introduced death so we could die and leave our sinful bodies, so Jesus Christ could come and die by shedding His precious blood on a cross, so He could be raised from the dead, and so we could spend eternity with Him.

The theory of evolution postulates cycles of death and struggle (bloodshed) over millions of years, eventually culminating in the emergence of man. The evolutionist sees today's world of death and suffering as a series of cycles, gradually evolving upward to higher and more complex levels, but the Bible teaches that the world we see is a cursed world. It is a world that was originally created in a perfect state by God, but has suffered the degenerative effects of the curse of sin, including the catastrophic effects of a global flood. Thus, evolution and the Bible (which, of course, includes Genesis) are in total conflict. The former would have us believe that death and bloodshed are the means by which man evolved. The Bible, on the other hand, clearly teaches that death — the result of sin — will be canceled, and man redeemed! The events recorded in Genesis are foundational to the Gospel message. The theory of evolution completely undermines the entire message of the cross.

21

In summary, if Adam were our ancestor, it means that God sets the rules, because He is the Creator. If, on the other hand, man's ancestor were an ape-like creature, and there is no God, then everyone has a right to their own opinions, and can set their own rules. If Genesis is not literal history, then Christianity has no basis for its doctrines.

Doubts about Genesis lead logically to doubts about other parts of the Bible, and ultimately, as we have seen, to complete unbelief. Again, this is because Genesis is foundational to the Christian structure.

How did these doubts arise, which have so undermined the foundations of the Christian faith?

Chapter 3 From Darkness to Light

Let us go back in time to a man who was very concerned about foundations, to a man who had no doubts concerning the infallibility of the Bible and the foundational importance of Genesis. On October 31, 1517, Martin Luther nailed his 95 theses to the door of the Wittenberg Cathedral in Germany. This marked the beginning of the Reformation. Martin Luther was a man who was concerned about foundations. He pleaded with the church of his day to return to the basic Scriptural truths — to God's Word as a basis for life. He recognized that Creation was a basic and vital doctrine. The Reformation he spearheaded was the beginning of man's emergence from the Dark Ages.

Martin Luther insisted that people could know truth because they had a revelation through the pages of the written Word — the Bible. Further, he showed that there was a simple way to discern false teaching with absolute certainty.

24

1517
MARTIN LUTHER
REFORMATION

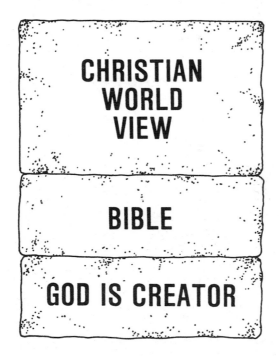

CHRISTIAN
WORLD
VIEW

BIBLE

GOD IS CREATOR

Because we have the Word of one who knows everything, when we build all our thinking on what He says, and not on the word of fallible man, we have a basis for determining what is correct. However, one of the basic problems down through history is that people have **not** accepted God's Word as truth. Instead, they have added their own opinions to the Bible, thus interpreting God's Word to suit their own desires. Of course, the church in Luther's time had done much the same thing; consequently, he placed great importance on returning to the proper foundation.

In my lectures, I often use the example of television murder mysteries to illustrate what is meant by the statement that only God knows everything, and that we must begin with what He says. No doubt you, too, have had the experience of watching such a mystery, and being sure halfway through the program that the butler did it. Three-quarters of the way through, it is still obvious that the butler is the culprit. Three minutes before the end, it's still the butler. Suddenly, you are given a lot of new evidence, which totally changes your conclusion. The butler didn't do it, after all! Because you did not have all the evidence, you came to the wrong conclusion. Alfred Hitchcock was a master of such plot twists. He built his reputation largely by frustrating his viewers with totally unexpected shocks at the end of his films.

Again, the only one who knows everything is God. Thus, it is only on the basis of what He says that one can come to right conclusions. Martin Luther certainly understood this point in the sixteenth century, and, of course, this realization revolutionized the church. As a result of this return to the proper foundation, many denominations were born which have carried evangelical Christianity through to the present. However, today the church has once again strayed from foundational truths. By-and-large, Christians are listening to the words of people who don't know everything, and who were not there when the world was formed. Consequently, their world view is not built on the right foundation, and their daily lives suffer.

A man with a wife and young family came to a series of lectures I was giving on this subject, and told me later how these talks had changed their lives. He had been experiencing relationship problems with his wife, and discipline problems with the children. After listening to the lectures, he decided to change his whole approach to these problems. The next time these issues arose, he said to his wife and children, "Okay, let's see what God says about this. Let's go to the Bible and obey God's rules, not our own opinions." His family was flabbergasted! But they listened. He then sat down with his wife and explained that both of them would have to obey God's roles and rules for the family, regardless of their own opinions. They knelt in submission before God, and from that point on, their family was built on the right foundation. What a difference this makes!

False Knowledge Condemned

True Knowledge Gained

A young Christian schoolteacher once confronted me after a meeting, saying that he felt children should be allowed to make up their own minds about things, that we should just lead them a bit, but not force them to think in any particular way. I handed him my Bible and asked him to show me where it said this was the way to teach children. He said he could not do that, but he still thought his opinion was correct. I asked him what had made him decide that this was the approach to use in teaching children. He explained that he had been brought up in a Christian home; however, he was forced to believe ideas thrust on him by his parents. Because of this upbringing, he later rebelled against Christianity, and it took him years to come back. He said he would not want his own children to rebel as he had done.

I then asked whether his parents had simply forced Christian doctrines on him, or whether they had given the foundation first (the reasons), and then built the structure of Christianity upon this. After thinking about it for some time, he admitted that his parents had not really given him reasons, and thus had not built the proper foundation for his faith. They had imposed a set of beliefs legalistically, without a basis as to why these beliefs were correct. He then realized why he had rebelled.

This story reflects a problem prevalent in both Christian and non-Christian circles. Most children are taught **what** to think, rather than **how** to think. They should be taught that their thinking is based on presuppositions. They must be taught why they believe what they do — what the basis is for their thinking. When taught this way, non-Christians realize the problem of trying to explain life on the basis of finite man's search for truth. Christians realize they can know truth, because they have the foundation of God and His revelation; thus, they have a reason for what they believe. As we will see, the evidence fits with revelation as it should. The young teacher speaking with me then realized that he must teach his children according to God's methods, not according to either his own opinions or the way his parents had taught him. His children would then learn how to think from a biblical foundation; they would have logical reasons for their faith.

Christians today no longer see the importance of interpreting Scripture **with** Scripture (not with human opinion). Scripture can interpret itself because it is the Word of God. The prevalent approach to the Bible today is to take one's opinions to the Word of God and tell God what He means! This is nonsense. We must take God at His Word and let Him tell us what is truth, and how we must think and live. If what He says disagrees with the opinions of fallible man, then man's opinion is wrong. We must be like Martin Luther — we must return to the proper foundation of our faith.

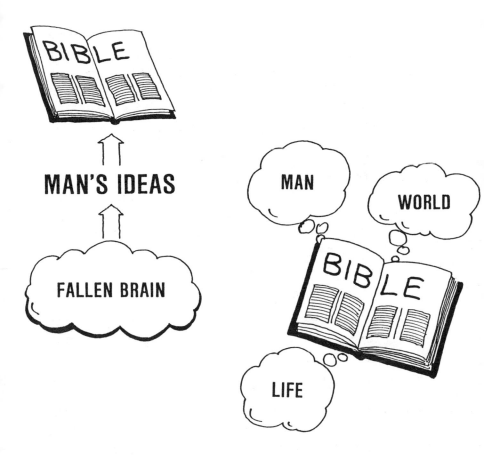

Consider the following chapter to see what happens when we add man's ideas to the Bible.

Chapter 4 The Compromise Road

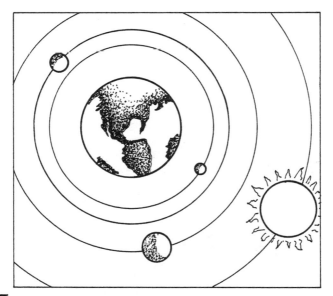

Many claim that the church historically has erred by interpreting the Bible literally rather than listening to the scientists who correctly explain Scripture. The example is given of Galileo as one who was persecuted by the church in the seventeenth century, because he disagreed with its dogma that the earth is the center of the universe. Many point to this case as an example of the church's involving itself in science based on the Bible and presenting its ideas as dogma, rather than leaving the scientists to discover truth. Thus, some say scientists cannot use the Bible as their foundation.

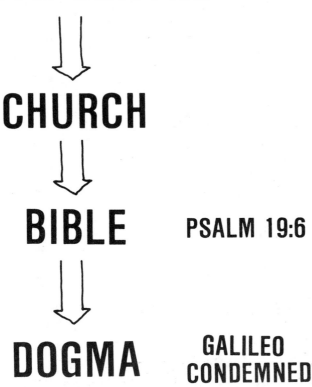

PTOLEMY
EARTH CENTRE

CHURCH

BIBLE   PSALM 19:6

DOGMA   GALILEO CONDEMNED

However, the whole Galileo affair has been misunderstood by many. What actually happened was that the seventeenth-century church had endorsed the view of Ptolemy (a follower of Aristotle) that the earth was the center of the universe. It then taught this idea as dogma on the basis of passages such as Psalm 19:6.

34

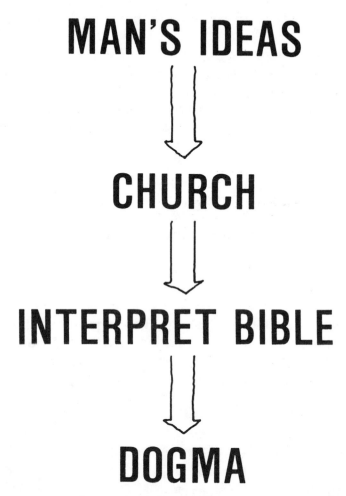

MAN'S IDEAS

CHURCH

INTERPRET BIBLE

DOGMA

In essence, then, the church had accepted a Greek idea and added it to the Bible. If, instead, the church had started with the Bible, it would not have taught that the earth is the center of the universe, for the Scriptures do not contain clear teaching on this subject.

Actually, there is another important lesson here. Although the Bible does not declare whether the earth is the center of the universe, it does contain clear statements of truth. For instance, we can teach as dogma that there was once a worldwide flood, for Scripture plainly states that the entire world was inundated by water in the time of Noah. Interestingly, the Bible further tells us that God put a rainbow in the sky as the sign of a covenant between Himself and man that He would never again send such a flood upon the earth (Genesis 9:9-16). There have been many floods since that time, but never a global one. We can be dogmatic about these things that are obvious from Scripture; however, when ideas are not clear, we should not teach our own opinions as dogma.

Some have claimed that the Bible should not be our foundation because it teaches errors, such as that the earth is flat, or is supported by pillars. But again, a close study of Scripture reveals that it states clearly that the earth is round and hangs in space (Proverbs 8:27, Isaiah 40:22, and Job 26:7). In all matters, Christians should be like the ancient Bereans of whom we read in Acts 17:11, "They searched the Scriptures daily whether those things were so."

It is very important to understand the distinction between what can be observed in the present and what has happened in the past. For instance, all scientists (Christian and non-Christian), because they agree on a language convention (i.e., they agree on the meaning of words, etc.), and because what they see and feel around them is real, can agree on what a fossil is. Many may even agree that the fossils are the result of catastrophic processes. Some may suggest that, because of the abundance of fossils, there was a global flood. However, to give meaning and proper historical content to the fossils would be impossible without the revelation of a witness to these events who had access to all knowledge. The Bible claims to be such a revelation from such a witness. Its record of the entrance of death into the world, and the event of a world flood, then, is a key to interpreting evidence in the present — connecting the present to the past. The biblical revelation is indeed foundational to our thinking.

The different approaches to connecting the present with the past can be seen in an event which occurred at the Grand Canyon. I heard an evolutionist guide tell visitors that "a lot of time and a little bit of water" caused the layers, and the eroded canyon. On the other hand, because of my access to biblical revelation (and because of the evidence of the present), I told the people on my tour that "a little bit of time and a **lot** of water" were responsible for the Grand Canyon. The evolutionist and I had the same evidence, but different explanations.

My revelation (the Bible) also tells us that the Creator God made all things; thus, the reality scientists accept exists only because of God. God is the ultimate foundation for all our thinking. However, because of the prevalent idea that the Bible is not foundational to our thinking, many Christians have made the same mistake the church did in Galileo's time. They have accepted as truth the word of fallible men who, though not having all knowledge, presume to tell God what His Word means. For instance, they accept the evolutionist account of how the fossils and such things as the Grand Canyon were formed, and then try to mesh these ideas with the Bible.

This error in thinking is reflected in the many compromise positions about Genesis which are held by various sections of the church today. Theistic evolution (the belief that evolution is true, but that God used this process), progressive creation (basically very similar to theistic evolution), the "gap theory" (postulating a gap of millions of years between Genesis 1:1 and Genesis 1:2), and many other ideas are prevalent today in Christian circles. Christians must be warned. The more one builds one's world view on the words of men rather than on the Word of God, the further one travels down the path to destruction.

Many Christians are quick to reinterpret the Bible when a scientist disagrees with what it says. However, when such a disagreement occurs, we should immediately consider three things:

1. What are the observable (using our five senses in the present), and thus obvious, facts we have in the present?

38

2. Are there some statements (concerning this evidence that supposedly disagrees with the Bible) that do not rely on direct observation, but require assumptions about the past? Do these statements include a framework attempting to put overall meaning to the facts? On what basis was this framework built? Can it be tested? If the answers to these first two questions are in the affirmative, and the basis for the framework is only man's theory, then it must be suspect, as man does not know everything, nor can he directly have observed events in the distant past.

3. Is my interpretation of Scripture correct? Is the conflict due to the wrong story being applied to the facts, or a wrong interpretation of Scripture? To sort this out, it is obvious that if the Bible is the revealed Word of the infinite God, then it must interpret itself; it must be self-authenticating. One should, without being influenced by external matters, attempt first to determine the context and true definitions of the words in the passage of Scripture being studied Then one should ask, "Is the subject referred to elsewhere in Scripture?"

Asking such questions will help determine which is wrong — the interpretation of Scripture or the external story about the facts. For instance, it is obvious that Genesis is a historical narrative containing the literal foundations of all doctrine. Thus, on these matters about which it speaks clearly, the book is authoritative.

For instance, if Christians used this method to interpret the Bible, they wouldn't have problems with the "days" in Genesis, Chapter 1. Many believe these days were long periods of time, perhaps even millions of years. However, if one studies the language of Genesis, the context of the passage in which the word "day" is used, and the references to this passage in other places in Scripture (e.g., Exodus 20:11), one can readily see that the Genesis reference is to an ordinary earth-rotation day. This subject is discussed in detail in Appendix One of my book *The Lie: Evolution*. The main reason people have not believed this definition of "day" is because they have taken the evolutionary belief that the earth is millions of years old, along with other erroneous ideas, and have attempted to fit these into the Bible. If, however, we begin with the Bible as our foundation and judge man's opinions on the basis of what it says, these problems will not arise.

Often, when we do start with the Bible, we are accused of having a blind, unscientific faith. I recall having a radio debate with a humanist about this matter. He declared that Christian scientists who use the Bible as their foundation are not real scientists. Real science, he contended, starts with doubts, which lead to theories that change constantly as new evidence is discovered. Because what the Bible says cannot be changed, he claimed it was, therefore, "unscientific."

He then admitted that, because he could never know if he had all the evidence, he could never be absolutely certain he had the truth. All he knew was that his theories would continue to change, and that the Bible was not right. He told me, "You start with the Bible, so you start with answers; whereas real science starts with doubts. You can't teach people answers because we never have all the evidence. You can only teach theories that are subject to change!" I then asked him why he could say the Bible was wrong when he had already admitted that he didn't have all the evidence, and therefore could never be absolutely sure about anything. In other words, how could he be certain the Bible was wrong when there could be a great deal of evidence he hadn't discovered, which would show it was right? What would he do then? He couldn't reply to this question. The point is that he, too, began with a preconceived idea; his foundation was the theory of evolution — and he was not prepared to change it.

At one church a young lady commented after my talk, "Well, that means I can believe it because God said it!" I replied that this was indeed the essence of what I was saying. However, don't fall into a trap here. Christianity is **not** just blind faith. We believe it because God said it, **and** because the evidence in the present clearly shows there is a creator. This evidence fits with what the Bible says, supporting our faith that it is indeed the Word of God as it claims to be.

One of the troubles with today's church is that many look on Christianity as a blind faith in which the experiential aspects count the most. However, if our basis for truth is simply our experiences (as it is for many Christians today), how do we know that we can trust our experiences? Others, outside the Christian faith, have experiences, also. Why shouldn't their "faith" be the correct one?

Chapter 5 Christianity is Unique

The uniqueness of Christianity is that the **evidence** is all there. We must be familiar with this evidence in order to give reasons for our faith (I Peter 3:15), to show that it is **not** just blind or experiential faith. Many Christians who are not familiar with the evidence for biblical truths regarding creation, and who see the humanists using "evidence" to support evolution, become anti-intellectual — not interested in evidence. Sadly, this anti-intellectualism in modern Christians often produces an unfortunate sequel in their children.

I have met many people who told me they rejected Christianity because their parents did not give adequate reasons to show that it was anything other than blind faith. Many have doubts about Christianity because they think Christians can't answer such questions as: "Where did Cain get his wife?" "Where did the races come from?" "What happened to the dinosaurs?" There are easily understood answers to all these questions which fit with the evidence and with the Bible. Please read the list of reference materials at the back of this book for the resources to answer these and many other questions.

I remember visiting a church in which the pastor told me, "I have never known how to answer the question about where Cain's wife came from, so whenever a man asked me this question, I would ask him why he was interested in someone else's wife! That usually put a stop to the question," he said. At another church, a woman said to the pastor, "I have often wondered where the dinosaurs came from." The pastor replied, "From mother and father dinosaurs!" While humorous, these answers reflect a very serious problem. In the eyes of the world, Christianity loses its power when its adherents cannot give answers to questions about the validity and trustworthiness of the Bible. Many books and research papers have been produced by creationist groups around the world to explain some of these seemingly difficult questions. They give overwhelming evidence in support of the accuracy of the statements in the Bible. Consider a few summarized examples:

1. Creation. I am often asked to give the evidence that there really is a creator. The answer is simple. Remember, if Romans 1:20 is correct ("For the invisible things of Him from the creation of the world are clearly seen, being understood by the things that are made, even His eternal power and Godhead; so that they are without excuse:"), then this evidence should be obvious to everyone. I remember when I was on a secular radio program, a caller asked me this question. Here's how I answered: "If **you** were looking for evidence of a creator, what would you look for? What are you prepared to accept? First of all, if you don't know what evidence you would accept, how would you determine whether what you were being given was truly proof of creation?"

Many have not thought through this question carefully enough. However, the answer is easy. If you are looking for evidence of a creator, you are searching for proof that there is intelligence behind all things which exist. Therefore, how do you recognize the evidence of intelligence? (As a schoolteacher, I used to look for the evidence of intelligence on the students' examination papers. A vain search it was, sometimes!)

Putting it practically, a radio station, for instance, does not exist because there was an explosion in a brick factory! Rather, intelligence (i.e., information), and a system to use the information, were involved in producing the station. Similarly, we know that the Presidents' heads carved on Mount Rushmore are not the result of millions of years of wind and water erosion. Intelligence and directed energy went into making those gigantic faces.

It is easy to recognize the effects of intelligence. When we look at life and consider the incredible amount of genetic information contained in each of our cells, we realize that the information in our genes must have come **from** information; it did not happen by chance. We **never** observe, anywhere in the world, functional complexity coming from disorder by random processes; there **is not one example**. Everything we observe with our five senses shows us that such order comes from disorder only when there is information (intelligence), and a system present to make it work. The evidence that there is a creator — a designer — behind this universe is overwhelmingly obvious. Anyone who does not believe in a creator is without excuse, even as Paul declares in the first chapter of Romans.

2. Worldwide Flood. Creationist geologists throughout the world have shown clearly that the fossil record is far more consistent with the catastrophic processes of Noah's Flood as recorded in Genesis, than with slow processes over millions of years. Whether coal deposits in Australia, obviously the result of billions of tons of plant material washed in by enormous quantities of water, or the hundreds of thousands of square miles of rock layers exposed to great depth at the Grand Canyon, the evidence fits with the biblical account of a global flood. Read the materials referenced at the end of this book for the exciting details of these examples, plus many more.

3. Origin of Races. The more scientists have studied the different races, the more obvious it has become that their origin fits with the biblical account of the origin of cultures and nations. All people of the world (except the rare albino) have the same color skin! Dr Gary Parker, in the book *What is Creation Science?*, explains that from a single pair (Adam and Eve), all the range of shades in skin color possessed by humans can be explained. This color is a reflection of the amount of the pigment melanin in the skin. A person with a great deal of this pigment, for instance, has dark skin. And converse-

46

ly, of course, a small amount of melanin produces a very light skin. The different shades of skin color, as well as other characteristics of the individual races, came as the result of division of the genetic pool at the time of the Tower of Babel. When God caused these men who had built the Tower to suddenly speak entirely different languages, the human race was immediately divided into different groups. The Bible tells us that all humans have the same ancestors — Adam and Eve. It is interesting to note that nearly every culture of the world — from Australian Aborigines to American Indians, Pacific Islanders, and Eskimos — has legends strikingly similar to the Creation and Flood accounts of Genesis. Of course, this is strong evidence which fits with the biblical view of the origin of the races.

After giving talks on the evidence for creation and Noah's Flood, I have seen exciting responses. Here is one example: A mature Christian woman told me that, previously, when non-Christians had challenged her on the issue of creation, she had told them it must just be taken by faith. She was so excited that she now knew that the evidence was on her side. It is faith, yes, but not blind faith. It is a faith which has the evidence, obvious to all who will see. Remember, Hebrews 11:6 states, "Without faith it is impossible to please Him: for he that cometh to God must believe that He is, and that He is a rewarder of them that diligently seek Him."

There is no way one can scientifically **prove** Creation

or the Flood, because those events occurred in the past. Nonetheless, if those events did occur, then the present evidence should be there — and it is. Christianity is such an exciting faith! Christ said that if the people would not believe Him for His Word's sake, they should believe Him for His **work**'s sake (John 14:10-11). He was telling His disciples that faith was necessary, but that the evidence was obvious. Christ said in John 11:42 concerning the raising of Lazarus from the dead, "And I knew that thou hearest me always: but because of the people which stand by I said it, that they may believe that thou hast sent me." He wanted them to see the evidence — the evidence that Christ was who He claimed to be: the Son of God.

In 1 Thessalonians 5:21 we are told to prove all things. Of course, in conjunction with this command is the fact that, as the Scriptures say, the Holy Spirit testifies with our spirit so that we **know** our faith is real (Romans 8:16, Galatians 4:6, 1 John 3:24, 1 John 4:13, 1 John 5:6). But all these things work together: faith, evidence, and the Holy Spirit. Oh, how the church needs to get back to faith in the Scriptures; back to building its thinking on the Word of God; back to the true foundation of Christianity — **back to Genesis.**

In the next chapter we will very carefully consider a blatantly obvious example of thinking built on the foundation of man's word rather than God's Word.

48

Chapter 6 The Path to Destruction

Consider the nations of France and England. In the eighteenth century, England experienced a great revival, and the Judeo-Christian ethic became the foundation of the fabric of society. France, meanwhile, underwent a traumatic revolution — a revolt against God and king. What was the basic underlying difference that caused such opposite results?

FRANCE

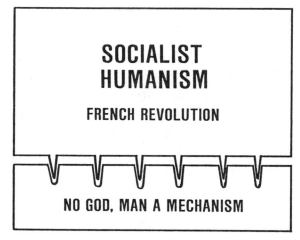

SOCIALIST HUMANISM

FRENCH REVOLUTION

NO GOD, MAN A MECHANISM

18th CENTURY

In France, the writings of philosophers such as Jean-Jacques Rousseau convinced many people that man was just a mechanism, and that the rules of society should be based on the general will of the people, rather than on God's laws. (Compare this with what was said in Chapter 2 about the theory of evolution and its effect on man's world view.)

What was the result of a totally man-centered foundation? The French Revolution of 1789. The stage had been set for men to declare that their rules should control society, not God's rules. This was the violent birth of pure socialistic humanism, and was in stark contrast to the American Revolution, which was founded firmly upon God as Creator. The opinions of those who could force their ideas on others became the rule for society. As Rousseau put it, people who did not agree with the majority should be forced to agree; they should be forced to be "free." Those who refused to agree were eliminated.

There are those today who hold similar views. We are told by modern liberals that we must tolerate all views. The truth of the matter is that these liberals tolerate all views **except** those of the Christians who say we must obey God's law. Our society dictates that we should be **free** to abort unborn children, **free** to be "sexually active" — even homosexual — **free** to teach only evolution, and **free** to employ anyone. If you don't agree, the courts will **force** you to be "free." Really, what is happening is that Christian absolutes are being systematically eliminated from society. People today are anything but "free."

The Bible, however, tells us what true freedom is: "... if ye continue in my Word, then are ye are my disciples indeed; and ye shall know the truth, and the truth shall make you free." (John 8:31-32) True freedom is knowing where you came from, who owns you, what is wrong with you, and what the solution is to the dilemma of sin. Rousseau's "freedom," like that of many today, is actually a bondage — a bondage to sin and its consequences. One of sin's consequences today is AIDS: the result of not being free, of not obeying the right rules about sex.

The world is being led astray by a lie. Far from becoming more and more free, the world is in fact falling more and more deeply into slavery to sin as it ignores the real foundation upon which its thinking should be built.

I became greatly intrigued by a young man I met once on an airplane. He said he belonged to a group that wanted to help bring good morals back into society. I asked what morals he meant. "Traditional morals," he replied. I asked what they were. By this time, he was becoming a bit frustrated! He emphasized again that his group wanted to see a return to good, traditional morals. I then asked if this meant Christian morals. He immediately said yes. I asked if it were a Christian group. He replied that it wasn't; that, in fact, two of the leaders were atheists! I asked him how atheists could insist that others have the same beliefs as they did; after all, if they were atheists, on what did they base their morals? What basis did they have for insisting that others have the same moral values?

The young man got the point. Without the right foundation, the structure cannot stand. So how can a society have Christian morals without a Christian foundation? Rather, a society with no such foundation would operate merely upon a set of opinions, and, because man is sinful, he would ultimately reject these opinions. This is exactly what has happened in our society. We have moved from freedom to bondage because we have lost the proper foundation upon which society should be built.

Chapter 7 Foundation for Family and Nation

In England, a very different "revolution" was taking place in the late eighteenth century. In fact, it was a momentous revival.

ENGLAND

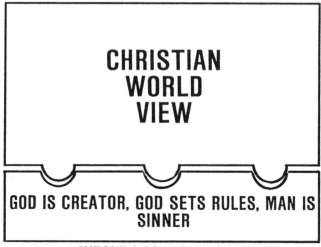

CHRISTIAN
WORLD
VIEW

GOD IS CREATOR, GOD SETS RULES, MAN IS
SINNER

WESLEY 18th CENTURY

Men such as John Wesley and George Whitefield had been preaching the Gospel, and the lives of thousands had been changed. They had experienced a relationship with Jesus Christ which assured them that the Bible was true. This relationship was not one of blind faith, however, as we have seen. Rather, many realized that the evidence around them

53

pointed to a creator. A watch demanded a watch-maker; more complicated things like animals and plants clearly pointed to an intelligent maker. To those who questioned further, it became obvious that it was Noah's Flood which had buried the billions of animals and plants — the fossils. The evidence was suddenly easy to see. The Bible could be trusted, not only when it spoke on history, but when it spoke on morality.

Thus, the foundation in England at this time became the Bible. Englishmen everywhere believed that one's world view should be built on God's Word. Society's rules for governing the people came from this absolute authority. People accepted these rules because they came from the one whom they knew had created them, and thus owned them, and who had also saved them from their sin. The fabric of society was basically Christian then, because the proper foundation existed.

This strong, Bible-believing community in eighteenth-century England, experiencing a vital relationship with the living Creator God, stood as a great barrier against any ideas of revolution against God and king. There was also a similar revival at this time in America, where Christianity with its inerrant Bible was the greatest obstacle to humanistic social philosophy. For such a Godless philosophy to succeed, a way would have to be found of eroding this barrier, and replacing it with a man-centered one (as in France).

54

First, public opinion would have to be changed concerning the truth of the Scriptures. To accomplish this, Satan would use the same method discussed in Chapter 1: bringing in doubt, which leads to unbelief. However, to cast doubts openly upon major doctrines of the Gospel message (e.g., the Resurrection and the Virgin Birth) would be immediately recognized as a direct attack on Christianity, and would be met with fervent opposition.

Let me give you a practical example. If one wished to destroy a building without those inside knowing it beforehand, one would not line up a number of bulldozers, tanks, and heavy artillery outside the building. The people inside just might look out the windows! But if one were to tunnel underneath to erode the foundations slowly but surely, the building would collapse before anyone inside knew what was happening. Termites provide another example. They can often erode the foundations of a building before anyone is aware of it.

The most subtle (and in the long run, successful) way to destroy this Christian barrier, then, would not be from the top down. It would be **from the foundation up.** For, obviously, if the foundation were eroded, the whole structure would ultimately collapse. In society, if Scripture were undermined, then man-centered reason would dominate. If unchecked, this erosion would eventually lead to the complete destruction of family and nation. Of course, this is exactly what is happening. And it all began with a subtle erosion of the foundation.

Chapter 8 The Erosion of Genesis

In 1795, James Hutton released his publication *Theory of the Earth*. Basically, its thesis was that in order to understand the geologic past of this planet, we must study the present earth and its processes. This approach, of course, was quite different from that of the many scientists who used the Bible as their foundation (including such things as the account of the world flood) to understand the earth's geologic history.

EXPANDED TIME FRAME

HUTTON 1795   LYELL 1830-1833

In 1830-1833, Charles Lyell published his *Principles of Geology*. Building on the work of Hutton, he promoted the idea that "the present is the key to the past." He proposed that geologic changes occurred slowly in the past, and, therefore, enormous time periods were required to form strata, mountains, and canyons. In other words, it excluded any consideration of **catastrophism**. [Catastrophism is the belief that massive upheavals (such as a world flood, along with the earthquakes, volcanic activity, and tidal waves that would have to accompany it) have been the major instruments in forming the geological features of the earth (rock layers, canyons, fossils, coal, etc.]. During such catastrophes, large forces acting at much greater rates than at present can do a tremendous amount of geological work in a very short time, something which the ordinary forces of erosion would require a very long time to do.

Lyell taught, as did Hutton, that the earth had been shaped by processes occurring slowly over millions of years. For instance, Lyell wrote that Noah's Flood was only a "tranquil" flood, leaving little physical evidence of its occurrence. He had already decided that the earth's vast sedimentary layers had been formed over long periods of time.

Even though Lyell at first appeared to believe in some sort of stability, there is actually a good deal of evidence to suggest that he had considerable influence in shaping his friend Darwin's views on evolution, which he later embraced openly. His published and private writings reveal a deep antagonism to the Bible from the beginning. He was a lawyer, not a geologist, and evolutionist Professor Stephen Jay

Gould, in his book *Ever Since Darwin*, described how Lyell used "true bits of cunning" and "imposed his imagination upon the evidence" in order to get his dogmatic, slow-and-gradual philosophy accepted as "the only true geology."

It is important to note that neither Hutton nor Lyell was viewed as directly attacking the book of Genesis. Rather, they subtly introduced doubts that its narrative could be taken literally. By popularizing the idea that the time frame for the earth was much greater than the mere several thousand years indicated by the Bible, they had cast doubt on the world flood of Noah's day, among other things. It was a very clever undermining of Genesis — the foundational book of the Bible. Once people could be made to doubt, it was much easier to bring them to a point of total unbelief, which is what Lyell wanted. Of course, there were also theologians who had been undermining the Bible in other ways at this same time.

And so, enough doubt had been created about biblical events such as Noah's Flood and Creation, that by the advent of Darwin's book in 1859, many people were fully prepared to reject the Bible's explanation concerning our origin in favor of a totally mechanistic, materialistic philosophy — secular humanism. This radically new belief system gradually replaced the eroding Christian foundation which had permeated the Western world following the Dark Ages, and had brought the laws of society into accord with biblical standards. As the foundation continued to erode, the whole structure above it began to collapse.

Because a new approach in determining the earth's geologic history was used to introduce the first major doubts about Genesis, this issue is still a crucial one. This approach — "the present is the key to the past" — is in essence a man-centered philosophy which rejects the Word of the only witness to all of history — God. Hutton and Lyell were really saying that revelation from finite man is the key to the past. This concept is an expression of their belief that man is autonomous — that he can determine truth by his own opinions (without biblical revelation). But was man present at the very beginning of the world? This question is exactly what the Lord asked Job: "Where wast thou when I laid the foundations of the earth?" (Job 38:4).

The Lord is teaching us not only the importance of revelation from the one witness who has always been, but also the limitations of man and his scientific method. People in Hutton's and Lyell's day by-and-large did not realize, nor do people today, that scientists cannot fully or directly investigate past events, simply because they have only the present evidence of these events. As God pointed out to Job, they were not there in the distant past. They cannot disprove any of the events in Genesis.

Neither can they prove scientifically the belief that hundreds of millions of years shaped the earth, since by their own philosophy no human observers were present during these supposed millions of years. However, the Bible records that God has always existed, and that He has given us a written record of exactly what did happen in the past, so that we may come to right conclusions about history. Simply put, then, **Biblical revelation is the key to the past** — particularly the past in regard to origins (Genesis, Chapters 1-11). Furthermore, the **past is actually the key to the present.**

Because many people in the late 1700s and early 1800s (particularly among the clergy) neither understood, nor even thought about, the limitations of the scientific method of determining the past, a considerable number of them accepted Hutton's and Lyell's theories, and reinterpreted the Bible. Let us consider some aspects of these limitations which should have been obvious to them.

1. Unique Events. If something has occurred only once in history, there is no way it can be proved in the present. For instance, many evolutionists believe life evolved from some primordial soup at a point in time millions of years ago. Such an event would be beyond scientific proof, as there were no witnesses and no written record. Even if such an event occurred today, it still would not prove that a similar event occurred millions of years ago. Some scientists insist that if they could create life from chemicals in a laboratory, such an experiment would prove that life could have evolved from chemicals. All this would really prove, however, is that it takes **intelligence** to make life — not chance.

6. Non-Measurable Evidences. If one cannot apply a measure to something, then it cannot be tested scientifically. For instance, when we look at the same sedimentary strata which Hutton and Lyell studied, we cannot measure the rate at which the layers were formed; they have already been deposited. Evidence from the actual strata (such as cross-bedding) may indicate rapid deposition, but because no scientist was there to see it happen, it cannot be proved scientifically. Thus, when Lyell postulated his "old earth" theory, people simply took his word — a human opinion — and decided that this was scientific fact. So non-measurable evidences are a problem which must be confronted by those who have accepted the evolutionist framework.

3. Assumptions About the Past. When it comes to the past, scientists cannot examine it; they have only the present. **All** the layers of the earth's sedimentary strata exist in the present. What many do not understand is that the geologic time-scale of evolution, ascribing millions of years to the various layers, is only a **story** about the past, based on the word of scientists who were not there! People assume that scientists have dug up a "Dinosaur Age," but all they have dug up are dead dinosaurs! The biblical revelation of a global flood provides a much better basis for understanding the origin of the strata and fossils. The evidence fits with this idea; however, creation cannot be proved scientifically either. But, using the scientific method in the present demonstrates that the evidence is consistent with biblical revelation, and **not** with evolutionist ideas. People should recognize that all scientists must begin with assumptions when they attempt to interpret the past. It's just a matter of which assumptions.

4. Absolute Negatives. When a scientist declares dogmatically that dinosaurs are extinct, this is a statement of belief, because one could never **prove** it. To do so, there would have to be someone at every point on the earth's surface to see that there were no dinosaurs. The point here is that no scientist has **all** the evidence. So how can evolutionist scientists claim that there was never a global flood? They were not there, and do not have all the evidence. God says He **was** there and **does** have all the evidence. If what He says about a worldwide flood is true, then the evidence should be obvious in the present — and it is! For more details, refer to the book *The Genesis Flood* by Dr. Henry Morris (listed at the end of this book).

5. Modern Dating Methods. Most people do not realize that modern scientific dating methods (which supposedly indicate a long age for the earth, thus "verifying" Hutton's work) are based on many invalid assumptions. Many creationist scientists have written on this subject in order to expose the incredible flaws in the methods used to date natural and man-made substances. For more information, refer to the book *The Biblical Basis of Modern Science*, listed at the end of this book.

In summary, the "age of the earth" issue was what began the erosion of the book of Genesis. Over a period of time, other factors (such as the hypothesis that it was actually written by a number of different men, rather than by Moses) helped to further undermine the first book of the Bible. People began to feel that they could no longer trust it. They had been fooled into thinking that the book of Genesis had nothing to do with science or, for that matter, with real history.

Chapter 9 The Pyramid Effect

How did this doubt in the book of Genesis spread? It is an obvious fact that in any organization — whether church, college, or government — the views of the person at the top are usually reflected all the way down through the organizational pyramid. What happened in the churches and church schools was that those at the top — theologians, professors, etc. — capitulated to the view that Genesis was not to be taken literally. This idea then gradually flowed down the rest of the pyramid, until those at the bottom were also indoctrinated. Consider a few specific examples in the church schools:

1. A "companion" to the book of Genesis (which claimed that Noah's Flood was only local), was published in 1841 by Dr. Samuel Turner, professor of biblical literature at the General Theological Seminary of the Episcopal Church in New York City. His students used this textbook and took this message to the churches.

2. Professor Franz Reusch, a Roman Catholic, taught the local flood concept at Bonn University in 1862.

3. James Dana, professor of geology (late 1800s) at Yale University, became a theistic evolutionist, influenced by both Charles Darwin and Asa Gray (a

Harvard professor of botany who, from 1860, became Darwin's promoter, ambassador, and apostle in the United States), and converted many students from the orthodox Christian position of Creation to the idea that God used evolution.

The students who had accepted compromising positions from their teachers eventually became professors and leaders themselves, convincing still others of their ideas.

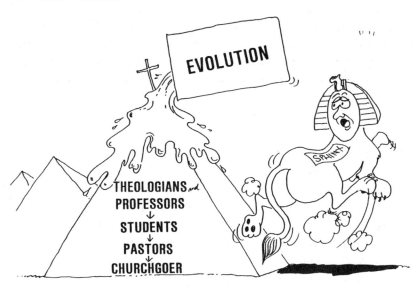

The clergy, then — as had the seminary professors — began to yield to theistic evolution, and accept the idea that Genesis was not meant to be taken literally. Their influence gradually filtered down to the general churchgoer, so that eventually most of them no longer felt that Genesis was literal — or even important — to either the rest of the Bible or to

Christianity. The destruction of the very principles of the Reformation, begun by Martin Luther in the sixteenth century, was now well underway. Doubt had led to unbelief.

I have conducted special programs called "Back to Genesis," which bring together people from many churches to hear the importance of this issue, and see the massive evidence in support of Genesis. Before each seminar, the local clergy are contacted by telephone in order to generate interest in the programs. Some respond very positively; however, some give answers such as, "We take the intellectual approach, not the simplistic approach of Genesis. Please don't bother us." What this really means is, "We take the human-opinion approach and reinterpret the Bible. We don't trust God's Word."

It should be noted that at the time Darwin's *On the Origin of Species* was becoming popular, many of the scientists who were Christians were standing against the idea of evolution. Well-known scientists, such as Faraday, Maxwell, Lord Kelvin, and others, would not accept the theory. There were also clergy pounding the pulpits, declaring that to accept the theory of evolution was to destroy the foundation of the Gospel.

However, then, as now, the press gave good coverage only to those who opposed the Bible and promoted evolution. By-and-large, people today are not aware of the media's anti-God bias, and their censorship of Christian thought. We hear and read only what the media want us to. I have so often found it true that when the media wish to make an issue of the creation-versus-evolution topic, they always find an opponent who claims to be a Christian, but who accepts evolution. The average radio listener, for instance, must surely be confused when hearing a debate in which one person, claiming to be a Christian, says evolution is an anti-God religion which destroys Christianity, while another person who claims to be a Christian (and is often even a pastor), advocates evolution.

I have been in situations in public schools in which a local pastor, after having given a lecture to the students on creation, then shared his personal point of view — **evolution**. How confused these students must be!

REINTERPRETATIONS

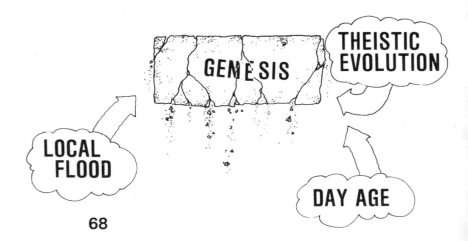

Unfortunately, there are many compromise positions in the Christian Church today which undermine the foundations of Christianity, such as theistic evolution, progressive creation, and the "gap theory," to name a few. These theories are discussed in detail in the excellent book *The Genesis Record*. See the listing at the end of this book to learn how to obtain this important publication.

One of the saddest aspects of these compromise positions is their effect on the younger generation. I have been to many churches and Christian schools which teach evolution. The effect is painfully obvious. The majority of students no longer have any respect for God's Word. In many ways their attitudes and actions are no different from those of people brought up in a completely secular environment. How dangerous it is to compromise the Word of God!

Chapter 10 The Generation Gap

Because people cry out for meaning and purpose to life (Romans 1:19 tells us that the knowledge of God is within us — we **all** know), the totally materialistic and mechanistic view of man does not satisfy. They need some mystical or supernatural element to replace the God whom they have rejected. Sadly, many today believe they have found this element in the "New Age" philosophy — the ultimate result of the destruction of the Genesis foundation. Once people are brought to this point, it is extremely difficult for them to change, because their mystical philosophy prevents them from being logical about reality. Satan is very clever — doubt does lead to unbelief — and he has brought about great degrees of unbelief. Once people have become as mystical as Eastern gurus, it is almost impossible to reach them with the message of salvation. This is the ultimate "generation gap."

I recall an incident that occurred at a seminar at which Dr. Gary Parker and I lectured. After our talks, three people came up to speak with us — a Hare Krishna devotee, a follower of the Baha'i faith, and an Eastern mystic. "Wonderful message," they said. I looked at Gary and whispered, "What did we do wrong?" We then talked with them, and no matter what either of us said, they agreed with everything. I realized that, because of their belief that everything is part of God, and that reality is whatever God is, then no matter what anyone said, or how inconsistent it was, they would always agree with it. It was quite difficult to make them understand the basics of Christianity. After all, how do you communicate with people in this real world when they don't believe in reality?

At the conclusion of another seminar, I met a man who told me, "I believe God is nature, and that we are a part of nature, and therefore a part of God." I then asked him where the matter came from of which nature is composed. He thought, and then said, "I believe in Noah's Flood, you know. But it wasn't worldwide — just local." I questioned him, "Where did you learn about Noah's Flood?" "From the Bible," he replied. "Well, the Bible makes it clear," I said, "that it was worldwide." He answered, "No, I don't believe that bit." He then thought for a moment and said, "I believe in the Ten Commandments, though." I asked, "Why?" "Well," he said, "they are the laws of nature." We went round and round. Here was a confused mind — a product of a modern education and mixed-up theological teachings. We were two human beings speaking the same language, and yet failing to communicate. There was definitely a "generation gap."

Chapter 11 Restoration, Reconstruction, and Revival

How can this "generation gap" be destroyed, and reawakening and revival brought about? I believe we must first concentrate on the church, rather than on the world. After all, is not the church the bearer of the message of salvation? How can the church continue its work if it is uncertain of its foundation?

Basically, Christians do not have a foundation for their position because of their compromises in regard to Genesis. How can the church tell the world they must believe the Christian doctrines and salvation message, when these are founded in a literal Genesis, and the church, on the whole, no longer believes in Genesis? How can we say God has created, when many Christians no longer understand what this means? If the church is lifeless, or even uncertain, how can it do this work?

I Corinthians 14:8 states, "For if the trumpet give an uncertain sound, who shall prepare himself to the battle?"

NO FOUNDATION

73

The church today must give that certain sound — the clear sound which shows that we know what we believe, why we believe it, and what the evidence is to substantiate it. Sadly, this is **not** the sound coming from much of today's church. It is an uncertain sound. Much of the church does not know what to say about evolution, Genesis, homosexuality, abortion, etc. They do not know what to say because they do not understand the very foundations of their faith.

GENESIS IS FOUNDATIONAL

Let us hear that certain, clarion note today that God is Creator, and that His Word can and must be trusted. Let us proclaim the truth, and call the church back to the Bible and **back to Genesis.**

The Bible-believing Christian can surely see the state of today's world — its wretchedness and unhappiness. But he should not be surprised. The world is in this condition because it is heedless of the message of Christ. We must be more concerned about the state of the church than about the state of the world. Why should the world take notice of the church if it does not see in the church the quality of life and certainty of position which attracts the world and convicts of sin? The church **must** return to its foundation.

Revival begins in the church. Peter tells us that judgment begins at the house of God (I Peter 4:17). In II Chronicles 7:14 we read concerning the Israelites, "If my people, which are called by my name, shall humble themselves, and pray, and seek my face, and turn from their wicked ways; then will I hear from heaven, and will forgive their sin, and will heal their land." This principle is just as applicable today as it was then.

Christians must realize how far short they have fallen from accepting the truth of God's Word — **all** of God's Word. The trouble is that the world is always trying to come between Christians and God. The more we listen to the world, the less we think of God. And, as Christians have listened to the words of sinful men who do not have infinite knowledge — men such as Darwin, Hutton, and others — they have changed what God has said; they have added man's ideas to the Bible.

Today's liberal Christians are promulgating the notion that changing times demand a changing Gospel. However, though we need to be sensitive to culture to a point, there is ultimately only one faith and one Gospel — as the Apostle John put it in Revelation 14:6, "the everlasting Gospel." And this Gospel has its foundation in the book of Genesis — the book of beginnings. The Christian Church will have no influence upon the world unless it holds to this faith of the apostles and presents the **truth**.

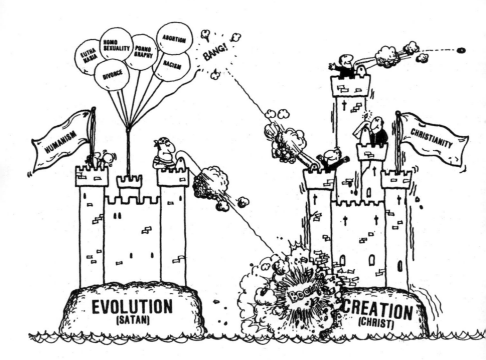

Sadly, too many churches and evangelists today are more interested in numbers than in truth. When I watch Christian programs on American television, though I see some excellent ones, more often I see evangelists intent, not on truth, but on numbers, flashy programs, power, and money. A great deal of Christian programming seems to be based on experiences rather than on doctrine; on surface issues rather than on foundational precepts. Such programs will not produce mature Christians who are able to cope with the problems of this world.

I am even concerned about some Christians who do believe the Bible in its totality. I have talked with certain evangelists whose meetings in large cities draw immense crowds, and have suggested how great it would be if a Creationist speaker were given the opportunity to tell such a large audience about the importance of Genesis, and the dangers to society's foundations from the theory of evolution. What has their response been? The replies have been that the creation ministry is too "divisive." It would split the clergy and lay people like no other Christian ministry, they say.

We must consider the fact that the ministry of Jesus Christ was divisive. In fact, He said He came to divide (Matthew 10:34). Let's face it — the truth is divisive! The writer to the Hebrews describes the Word of God as "quick, and powerful, and sharper than any two-edged sword, piercing even to the dividing asunder of soul and spirit, and of the joints

77

and marrow, and is a discerner of the thoughts and intents of the heart;" (Hebrews 4:12). And God's Word **includes Genesis.**

These same evangelists have told us that allowing creationists to speak at their meetings would cause them to lose a lot of support, thereby preventing them from reaching thousands. My reply to this is, "In the long run, isn't it more important to teach the people the truth about God, and make sure they build their faith on the right foundation? Isn't that the most important thing for the future of this nation?"

Many pastors and evangelists, however, **are** taking a stand on the creation issue, and the Lord is blessing their work. So let us as a body of believers go back to representing truth, the whole truth, and nothing but the truth. Let us get **back to Genesis.**

The following diagram summarizes what Christians can do. It is a challenge to the church!

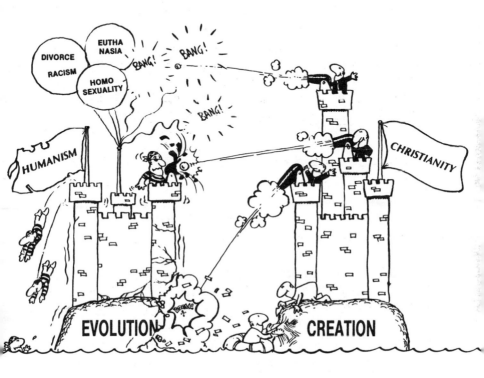

List of Recommended Further Reading

The Lie: Evolution, K. Ham, Master Books, El Cajon (CA), 1987, pp. 168.

A layman's guide to establishing a truly biblical way of thinking about the whole area of origins, and restoring the foundations of Christianity.

The Genesis Record, H. Morris, Baker Book House, Grand Rapids (MI), 1976, pp. 668.

A verse-by-verse devotional and scientific commentary on the whole book of beginnings — a MUST for Christians serious about their faith!

The Biblical Basis for Modern Science, H. Morris, Baker Book House, Grand Rapids (MI), 1984, pp. 516.

The most detailed one-volume analysis of all aspects of creation/evolution.

Bone of Contention, S. Baker, Creation Science Foundation Ltd., Brisbane (Qld), 1980, pp. 35.

A layman's summary of the scientific arguments for creation.

What is Creation Science? H. Morris, G. Parker, Master Books, El Cajon (CA), 1982 (1987), pp. 331.

A more detailed, semi-technical study of the biological and physical aspects of creation science.

The Long War Against God, H. Morris, Baker Book House, Grand Rapids (MI), 1989, pp. 344.

A scholarly, yet intensely readable documentation of the whole sorry history of evolutionism, back into ancient history, and before.

The Answers Book, K. Ham, A. Snelling and C. Wieland, Master Books, El Cajon (CA), and Creation Science Foundation Ltd., Brisbane (Qld), 1990, pp. 144.

Detailed answers to the 12 most common questions about creation and evolution. Illustrated.

The above books can be obtained from:

> Master Books
> P.O. Box 1606
> El Cajon, CA 92022 USA

> Creation Science Foundation Ltd.
> P.O. Box 302
> SUNNYBANK, QLD, 4109, Australia

Creation Magazine, Creation Science Foundation Ltd., Australia.

A unique quarterly family magazine with a special children's section. Specializes in refuting evolution and giving faith-strengthening and witnessing ammunition. Obtain from:

U.S.A. — P.O. Box 710039, Santee, CA 92072 USA

or

Australia — P.O. Box 302, Sunnybank, Qld, 4109